Love,

Deborah

!Shut Up!

An Ancient Mantra for Complete Happiness

(The Simple Truth Your Guru, Therapist,
And Grandmother Forgot to Tell You)

Dvorah Adler
Art of Living Foundation Books

!Shut Up!

An Ancient Mantra for Complete Happiness

Copyright © 2005 by Dvorah Adler

Edited by Laura Weinberg, Michèle Krolik and Martina Straub

Published by Art of Living Foundation

ISBN: 978-1-885289-10-3

Cover and book design: Andrew Behla and Dvorah Adler
Front cover photo of Dvorah and inside photo of Sri Sri:
Ron Weinberg
Back cover photo: Melissa Weisfenning

Published by:
Art of Living Foundation
P.O. Box 50003
Santa Barbara, California 93150-0003
United States of America

More products are available through:
Art of Living Bookstore
www.bookstore.artofliving.org

Dedication

I dedicate this writing and all that I am to that One who has brought me out of the confusion and misery of life, to Love, the sweet home that I Am. That One that is my very self, my very best friend, and most darling adorable Guru of my heart. I am That. He is That and plays in This like no other. He is truly a great mystery to me... I honestly just don't get Him. All I can do is go deeply into That which has no face or name or feeling, and be at home with Him. But understand Him? Impossible!

Darling, darling, darling Sri Sri, what can I ever say to you? In all adoration, I bow deeply to your vastness and sweetness of form. And in deep adoration and devotion, I often whisper your name, making faces in the mirror to amuse you. I love you, my most precious darling, dear One.

Your darling, adorable Dvorah

"The Master is like a window. There is a body and a frame. But through him you can get a glimpse of the infinite, the vast expansion of the sky. The highest flowering of divinity in manifest form."

–Sri Sri Ravi Shankar

Special Thanks…

I want to thank my most adorable precious children, Todd, Torah and David, for being my inspiration and loves on this path of life… They've understood me like no one else, and have accepted, supported and chuckled lovingly at my outrageous, eccentric personality and hilarious antics.

And of course, I'd like to thank my Art of Living family, who in His name, have always made me feel welcome. Thank you…

"Silence is the totality of the mind. In it, the other disappears. Be quiet for awhile."

–Sri Sri

Contents

Forward

My dear, adorable family of friends: I woke up this morning and had to write this book. It's because of my immense love and adoration for you that I can't keep this burning ancient secret inside of me any longer.

Over time I see you unhappy, in pain, dissatisfied, complaining and regurgitating your latest psychological and spiritual catastrophe and I want to whisper the good news in your ear: "Please, darlings, please, relax. Breathe the fresh air that you are and please, please, sweet ones, relax." And when that doesn't work, I'd like to breathe the truth that you are into your pores, so that it floods your system with the sweetness of love and you finally come to rest in the arms of yourself.

Unfortunately, all my whispers of sweet nothings haven't worked. Only a few of you have warmed to my embrace and joyful chiding and are living, loving, and laughing your life.

The rest of you are stuck with your unhappiness and ungrateful whinings. "When will I feel better, more whole, more enlightened? Why do I make the same mistakes over and over again? When will I ever learn?" After months and years of meditation, affirmations, and therapy work, "Why do I still have negative thoughts and feelings? Why can't I be more grateful? Why don't my relationships last? Where is my soul mate? Why can't I live in the 'now' and let go of my past, and stop worrying about my future? When will I finally be happy? (And the big one...) What am I doing wrong?"

These questions have kept you churning in your own wheel of misfortune and deadly hope. But, hey, it's okay, I love you, and you're in luck, the honeymoon is over. We're way past all the playful teasing and whispers of loving endearments. It's time to drag you home, by your hair if need be, so you can finally get what you've been begging, pleading and crying for—a little peace, in the land of milk and honey. Your sweet, ever lovin', most adorable Peace that you are.

So now, sweethearts, open your mind, body, and soul, and take a deep breath in—and let it out. It's time for the big secret of the ages, the true words of the Gurus, Avatars, therapists, healers and wise grandmothers. This is what they've always wanted to say to you, but were afraid of losing their adoring followers and family of friends, or perhaps it just wasn't their nature... So, my darlings, ready? Repeat after me:

Shut Up! And be Happy!

When Will It Get Better?

Okay, my dear Ones, let's check out the first pressing question that's always on your mind, "When will it get better?" It's hard to believe that after all your failed attempts at getting and staying in balance, searching for the right magic crystal, course, shaman or formula to make you permanently happy or enlightened, you're still moaning, groaning, barking, begging, bowing, pleading, pretending, praying, cajoling, hoping, and giving your nonexistent fortunes away, for the mere possibility of "finally, finally, after all these so-called lifetimes, being free, happy and enlightened."

Well, let me be the first to give you the good news. Your life, as you live it, or as it lives you, will never ever get permanently better. I know you want it to get better forever, and you pray for it to get better forever, but darlings, forget it!!! It ain't gonna to happen! So please stop blaming yourself because you're not meditating enough, fasting enough, or chanting enough to get rid of all your stress and bad karma. And please, don't be so egocentric as to believe that your inability to keep it together is stopping the Age of Enlightenment, heaven on earth, nirvana, Christ's Second Coming, Matreya, Babaji or the Ashtar Command from coming to save the earth.

Darlings, Wake up! You're tripping...living in misery and drugged on possibilities. Your only real hope is to stop hoping. Be where you're at! That's the real secret, the illusive, so-called hidden secret the world doesn't want you to know, for fear you might start having a really good time. You've been so busy "looking and hoping for love and fairy tales in all the wrong places," that you're missing your life, your fun, and your true calling to be thriving and happy in spite of problems.

Now you're always philosophizing and talking about being here now, or living in the present moment, "yada, yada, yada." Unfortunately, most of you are only pretending to accept and live in the moment. In reality you're waiting for the car in front of you to hurry up, so you can get home to dinner and your favorite DVD.

If you could just accept the fact that This Is It, This Is Really It, there is nothing but this very moment, this ordinary, mellow, deep, big, vast, beautiful, dripping with honey, oscillating orgasmic sour apple pie holy space moment you've been looking for. Then maybe, with a little bit of luck or grace (whichever you believe in) you'd finally give up this hope, this absurd, unfulfilling notion of "better" and chuckle, screaming ecstatically at the jerk in the car in front of you. You'd finally be free to really enjoy the moment, even if it meant being stuck in gridlock traffic.

I tell you, adorable Ones, it's a good life when you give up this fantasy and start living!!! Start being satisfied with what's happening, instead of waiting and praying for the next moment to happen. Stay open to the possibility that everything is exactly as it Can Only BE. And that if it could be different, it would be different. Then you have a real chance at some happiness and peace. A real taste of that "Big Yum" you've been "hoping" for and doing all those good deeds for.

My advice to you is to stay in your room or go to a park. Suck your thumb or lick a lollypop. Watch TV or feed the birds. Drink a glass of wine or eat ice cream. Just make sure that you do whatever you want and do it guiltlessly. If you'll notice, the world (as it is, good and bad) goes on effortlessly without you and your constant prayers for peace, help and management.

If you end up sending Aunt Mary or Mother Earth some good wishes, great–but if it doesn't come up, don't start feeling guilty and useless about it. Apologize or don't. Either way, let it go, because you couldn't help it. The moment and all the circumstances surrounding that moment brought about a specific (non-changeable) action. And frankly, it had nothing to do with you, because it was a thought, feeling or action in time that you had no control over. If you start taking responsibility for every ridiculous thought, feeling or action you've had, then you'll really start cooking in your own miserable juices of loss and regret and be right back where you started—in confusion and unhappiness.

I know it may seem irresponsible to you to think this way, but life does live you (strange as that may sound). The control you think you have is an illusion—a phantom belief the world and those close to you have led you to believe. Unfortunately, you've bought into it and are still miserable, out-of-control, and wondering why you can't be more responsible.

If you would just notice that things "happen as they happen, and are as they are," you'd move from one moment to the next without this constant despair, blame, and "what if." You'd shriek with awe at the sheer lunacy of your drama. It's a billion-dollar movie that only a master scriptwriter could craft.

So, my dear darlings, cheer up. Drug yourself on a little "as is-ness" satisfaction and "okay-ness," instead of the usual affirmations and hopeful distractions. Peace and happiness may catch up with you, when you stop trying so hard to find them.

Why Do I Make the Same Mistakes Over and Over Again? When Will I Ever Learn?

All right, darlings, here we go again–bemoaning ourselves. Somewhere along the line, you were led to believe that you were different from the rest of world, the rest of nature. You see the flowers bud, bloom and wither. You watch the tide roll in and the tide roll out. You see winter change into spring, then summer, fall, and winter again. You observe the history of the world and people repeating themselves time and time again, and you wonder, "When will they ever learn?"

Volcanoes erupt, calm down, and then periodically erupt again. War breaks out, peace prevails, and then war breaks out again. This persistent reoccurring pattern should give you a hint into your own ever-changing reoccurring condition, but it doesn't. You still don't get it. You marvel in discomfort, "When will I ever learn? When will I stop going through these cycles of depression, optimism, anger, patience, clarity, denseness, expansion, and contraction? When will I stop this constant changing back to the way I don't want to be, making the same mistakes, over and over again? When will I finally get it?"

My Dears, stop breaking your head over the natural order of things. Stop bucking the tides, the earthquakes and the seasons of time. Look around you. It's all changing constantly and it "seems" to be changing in cycles. A star explodes, a star is born and explodes again. A man dies, a man is born and then dies again. A feeling wells up, a feeling subsides and wells up again. A thought comes, a thought goes, and here it comes again. It all seems to be coming and going, and no one knows where.

The only thing we're all sure of is that it's changing all the time, and it appears to be in a familiar pattern, i.e. "There is nothing new under the sun." Now, how many times have you heard or said this mantra? Many, I'm sure. Yet you don't make the connection, you don't take it to heart. It's the rhythm of your mind, body, and soul. It's the rhythm of your life. You are not different from all the events and movements that take place around you.

You are made of the same spiritual and chemical gel as the rest of the world. Your cells are forever dying and regenerating, and you are part of the continuous modulation and recurrence of "What Is." Your mind, body, and spirit echo themselves, repeating their thoughts, actions, and divine experiences indefinitely, until your homecoming. And then...it still continues, but you are very, very, very cool. You're in the translucent moment, the empty, vast, bigness of "What Is." You're finally comfortable, at peace, with your mess and flow of life. You're home.

Until then, you will continuously ask the same disconcerting questions, "Why do I make the same mistakes over and over again? And when will I ever learn?"

To that I say, "Who knows and who cares?" Live your life and be at peace. All your wishes, hopes, prayers, and hard work to change yourself are useless in the face of What Is. It may go your way or it may not. Either way, relax or don't. Just be at peace with What Is.

After All My Meditations, and Therapy, Why Am I Still So Angry?

My darlings, how long have you been trying to get rid of your anger? Yet, it still persists and comes up again and again at the most unexpected times. You just finished your meditation, affirmation, or prayer, and the phone rings. It's a pesky bill collector or your boss mentioning your latest transgression—and off you go again. Although you may have controlled your anger outwardly, inwardly you're still a little itchy, irritated, and churning.

Maybe you didn't outwardly express your anger at the time, but when the cat suddenly rushes by, you start yelling unexpectedly, "Hey, what are you doing, you dumb cat? Watch where you're going!" That's when you realize you've broken another promise to yourself. You just can't control your anger. You feel about as trustworthy as the weather.

Look, dears—can you control the sun? Can

you control your nose when it twitches or your eyes when they well up with tears? It's your system and it does what it was meant to do. And this system has a twitch called anger. Now sometimes it "appears" as if you can control it, but basically, it just comes and goes like everything else, and you're left wondering what happened after the storm.

So now, please tell me, after all of your prayers and hundreds and thousands of dollars spent on courses meant to control your anger, is it finally gone? Are you a "cool, collected cucumber" or maybe a "high unemotional Zen zombie?"

Chances are you're neither. You're probably still trying to keep it together, all the while wondering what you're doing wrong, and why you still can't shake your anger.

So again, may I offer a bit of my favorite advice? "Shut up! and Be Happy!" and may I add, "Wake up already!!! You're dreaming misery!" Anger is part of this system, and as long as you're alive (which in itself is debatable), anger will arise at one time or other.

When anger does come, fine, accept it. Shout a little or a lot, dance a little or a lot, cry a little or a lot, or even throw a tantrum. But eventually a little awareness will dawn, and your anger will subside, like everything does. Then you'll be able to go on your merry way again, until the next time and the next and the next time. Now let's be honest, wasn't that fun???

Unfortunately, where you screw up, my darlings, and make yourself miserable, is when you take your anger so personally, and go on bemoaning your unenlightened fate. So again, let me reiterate, "Anger comes and anger goes, and that's the nature of life."

So, for God's sake, my darlings, do shut up and stop this continuous cycle of blaming and misery. And please, please, have a little mercy on me, because you're giving me a headache. How much love do I have to pour into your system before you decide to let a little peace into your life? How many times do I have to shout, "I love you, I love you, I love you, I love you a trillion, zillion times" before you finally giggle in ecstasy?

Honey buns, anger is fun! It's energy. It

brings peace and calm to your body. It's a gift, like love, compassion, and Haagan Das, so stop trying to get rid of it. Embrace it. Honor it. Make a monument to it. Put the names of all the people from the beginning of time on it that couldn't control their anger. Then you'll see that no one is left out and you're in good company. Just think of it. You and your anger are part of the history of mankind. Pretty cool, huh?

Now most important of all, it's time to stop being afraid of your anger. It's not going to manifest anywhere it's not supposed to. You're not suddenly going to ruin your life, destroy your family, the world, or offend your God or Guru, with your fantasies, negative wishes or desires. If it's going to happen, there is nothing you can do to stop it. Because, my darlings, it just isn't your game. And in the face of The Game "What Is," you are powerless.

So, relax, and stop blaming yourself every time a little twitch of anger shows up. Be happy. Stick your tongue out at anyone you want to, but be sure to apologize, apologize, and apologize. That way you can stick your tongue out again and again and again.

Why Can't I Be More Loving?

BECAUSE YOU CAN'T! Why can't you understand that? You're as loving as you can be, and that's it! You're always trying to buck the tide, always wanting everything to be different than what it is. That's what makes you so miserable–your chronic unhappiness about what is, what's happening in your life. You constantly want it to be different. Open your eyes, all your eyes–see with a little contentment. It's not better anywhere else but HERE.

You're always battling with love. You want to love more, you want to be in love, you want everyone to love each other, you want everyone to love Mother Earth, you want the world to be made of love, act like love and hopefully (there's that word again) become love. You're infatuated with love. You might as well be infatuated with a Halloween mask. It's the same difference.

Love to you is an object, something to

aspire to, something to possess, something to become. Again, it's a crazy notion that someone stuck in your head and you're so charmed by it, it's kept you stuck forever. Let me help unglue you. Love is not an object, not something you can become. It's You. It's your very Nature. It's the stuff that everything is made of. You're already love, so you can stop trying to become it. Don't you get it????? Let me repeat: YOU ARE LOVE. Period.

Don't think about it. Just relax, take a breath, be still, and stop this incessant search for love. It's just plain dumb, and you're very intelligent. Your search for love has brought you nothing but disappointment. Tell me, has love ever satisfied you? It's so fickle, it changes so often, and you can't ever get enough of it. It always leaves you wanting, longing, and praying for relief. When was the last time you were in love, in that hunger of love? It took over your entire system, and for what? Only to be crying and moaning with disappointment later. From your boyfriends and girlfriends, to your husbands and wives, to your parents, to your children and even to your Guru—you've been agonizing about love. Enough already! Wipe your tears! You've been banging your head against the wall and forgot to put the timer on so you could remember to stop.

I am Here. I'm your timer. STOP! IT'S ENOUGH! Love is not an emotion, it's not your latest thought or fantasy. It is your very Nature. You are Love. Now repeat after me, again and again and again, "Love is my very Nature. I am Love."

It's amazing what happens when you recognize who you are. You begin to have some peace in your life. You stop trying to convince yourself and the world about what they "should be doing" to become more loving. You recognize that they are love and that becomes the grounds for true communication. You begin to love from a different perspective. You stop trying to convince everybody to love you. You become free of the chains of love and become a beacon of love. You can't help it. No effort. It's your Nature.

It may sometimes appear as if you can't stand someone or something, but honestly, it's on the very surface, like dust on your computer.

You may react negatively to someone, but it's the circumstances of that situation. In truth, you are love to each other, and all your shouting and rude words and actions fall flat in the face of LOVE. So, be easy. Don't fret about your challenges with love. It's only your playful concern made into a big deal.

Be sweet with yourself. Love is inevitable... Sorry, there's no getting away from it. It follows you wherever you go. You don't have to search for it or confuse yourself with it. It just is, like your lovely eyes. My darlings, how can I tell you how much I love you? Oh, Love, sweet love, so charming and so completely YOU.

Why Can't I Get Rid of My Ego?

Darlings, you don't have an ego. Who told you that you had an ego? What you have is a case of the blues. You imagine you have an ego, and in the name of that fantasy, you cause yourself all kinds of havoc. You imagine all kinds of transgressions in the name of your imaginary ego, and then you hold everyone else responsible for their miserable egos too. What an egotistical life you've structured!

The ego you've manufactured is just another one of your games to keep yourself interested in life. What would you do without an ego to keep you occupied?

It's your preoccupation with your ego that keeps you busy and challenged, as you search out different ways to get rid of it. Think of all the time and money you've spent on self-development classes, just so you can keep your ego in check. And notice how unhappy and desperate you get when your "ego" has sabotaged your life, especially when you're finally getting somewhere on this spiritual path.

My dear, it's ridiculous how much attention you give to this "idea" called an ego. It's another one of those illusions that keep you bound in hope and worry. You hope you'll be able to conquer it, and you're worried you never will. It's quite a loop you've gotten yourself in.

So, my darling, here comes more good news. You can drop all that useless worry about your ego and live life as if you've conquered it. You can be the master of your ego. How does that make you feel–happy?

I want you to shout out loud at this moment that you're free of your ego. As a matter of fact, I'd like you to announce to the world that you're madly in love with your ego. Tell them your ego is now your very best friend and you don't know how you ever thought of living without it.

Design a big Kali statue ego of yourself, with gorgeous exotic flower leis around your neck, and buy an exquisite silk sari to wrap about your beautiful body. You now have a stunning ego you can truly worship and adore, just like the holy statues in the Vedic Temples.

You see, once you finally get over your baseless fear of your ego, you're finally free to laugh and enjoy your life. You'll probably start boasting and telling everyone how wonderful, intelligent and beautiful you are. Everyone will begin to marvel at your huge, gorgeous, over-the-top ego.

My darlings, what a trip you are, such a precious, adorable trip. Why would you ever want to get rid of your ego—such a huge, shimmering in-your-face ego? Have fun with it now. Kiss and embrace your ego. Let it play with the other glorious egos in your dream universe.

Why Can't I Serve More Instead of Being So Lazy?

My darlings, many of you are obsessed with service, like you're obsessed with "doing things right," another thing to drive yourself crazy with misery. Service is your very Nature. How can you be anything but service to What Is? That's all that's happening.

However, if you're lucky enough to have service (natural activity) come your way, then yes, leap into action. Do the dishes, help that little old lady across the street, play with those children, collect money for the less fortunate, lay yourself on the wet asphalt so your girlfriend's shoes don't get wet. But, darlings, if it doesn't come up, don't fret and go into a panic. Feeling useless because you're not serving doesn't serve anyone, especially you. It only puts you in a funk of feeling miserable and serving even less.

You still have this illusion that you're going to hell or a miserable next lifetime if you don't do the "right thing" and serve, serve, serve. You cause yourself endless concern over your inability to hop to it and serve the universe.

Well, darlings, relax, you've been duped again. You are service, and if it doesn't come up, it just doesn't come up. What good does it do to break your head over a concept of service? It doesn't make you serve any more does it? Think about it. The Guru told you to do something. You want to do it, you have all the intention of doing it, you plan to do it–but you don't do it. Why? Because!

Who knows why? All you know is that it didn't happen. So now you blame yourself, flag-ellate yourself over something that JUST DID-N'T HAPPEN. Forget it! It didn't happen; go on to the next thing. Service will always come up, and if your Guru doesn't tell you what to do, then your mother or life will. You'll have plenty of chances to serve your heart out. Meanwhile, "Shut up and be happy!" Stop whining about how lazy you are and can't do anything you're supposed to. If you're supposed to do it, you will.

Now, darlings, people have different

natures. Some can't stop serving, while others need a canon lit under them to get up and answer the door. Either way, it would be generous of you not to judge other people's disposition towards service. We all do what we can, and your judgments only make you more miserable. If you do grumble, that's fine. Just don't get stuck in it like everything else. Know it for what it is, "a grumble in time" and move on!!

My darlings, you need to relax about your life, whether it's service or something else. It's not your fault or anybody else's, so get out of the blame game. If you can't stop blaming it on yourself, then blame it on your Guru (he can take it). Or better yet, blame it on the weather, and if that doesn't work, then blame it on the angels of the West or maybe of the South, whichever bothers you the most. But please, stop blaming it on yourself. It doesn't serve you. You are Service.

How Many Past Lives Have I Had, and How Many More Do I Need To Finally Be Free?

Darlings, why can't you just live in ME, instead of constantly trying to find another place to go, another distraction to drive yourself crazy with? Come to Me—think of me, instead of another piddly life of misery and illusion. I am your life—the only one you've ever had. Live in me and dream of ecstasy, space, and the yummy coolness of the unknown.

Why can't you drop the fantasy of better worlds, better lives and better experiences? Live in me and live in peace, without the constant bother with mind-boggling concepts like other lives? What do you know of other lives? Nothing. You know nothing, absolutely nothing, regardless of your "past life experiences" and techniques.

You've just played with your own mind, making up stories about your unhappiness and past exploits. Honestly, you're crazy with thoughts of nonsense. I'm offering you such love, such innocent pure devotion. You'll never have to break your head, wondering about longing and why can't I love more and how can I be more devoted to my Guru, to my practice and to other people. I am offering you peace, deep, luscious, in-your-face peace. Why can't you hear me? I want you to stop fantasizing about nonsense, and finally, take a leap of faith and live in Me.

If you really want to know about how many lives you've lived and how many lives you've got left, better go to someone who knows about such things, because I know nothing about it. How can space reincarnate into anything? But your mind can reincarnate into whatever, whatever, and whatever...and I'm not interested in whatever. I'm interested in What Is.

Darlings, again, give up all these fantasies of known places. They're known and so boring, and in the end, they're just another circle, another rectangle, or another square. And, "Oh, isn't it great, here comes another triangle, but, oops, it doesn't look like a triangle, it looks like a hat! Whoopee, I saw a hat!" Why do you want to look at a hat from 1000 different perspectives? It's not enough that you've seen and felt a hat in this life a million times. Now you want to see a hat in different colors and styles and textures, ad infinitum… And after that, you want to paint it, study it, and go around the hat circle again so you can review what you've already seen.

Enough, my darlings. Wake up! Wake up! Wake up! You're dreaming, and all you're doing is dreaming of more and more interesting triangles that happen to look like hats. Soon you'll start on the squares that look like boxes, and the rectangles that look like windows, finally fascinating yourself with circles that remind you of chakras…until you bore yourself with every shape in the stratosphere.

I offer you fresh, uncharted territory, something always new and fresh. You will barely know what's in front of you until you see it for the first time, and then you'll get so excited, like a child with his first Christmas tree. No more regurgitated lifetime hats. Just this life, this miraculous, awe-inspiring life, with its fresh kaleidoscope of colors, shapes and sizes—all readily available to be lived, giggled and enjoyed in Me.

Now, darlings, don't you think it's time to imagine me. Feel me. Adore me. Kiss me. Breathe me. Love me. And then you'll see what happens to all your questions of other lives and other repetitive experiences. They'll wither and fade into the ether where they came from. In their place will flow the depth and breath of yummy, yummy, yummy Me.

So, come darlings, take a leap of faith and dive into this translucent, cool blue pool of love, Me. I will love you forever, cherish you forever, and adore you forever, through every lifetime fantasy you've ever dreamed of.

I'm yours, you're mine, and the biggest surprise of all—is You. It's all you...through the entire history of mankind, through the millennium of time, century after century, yuga after kali yuga, there has only been One. There has only been YOU.

So now, darling, tell me, what was your

question again? Who did you think you were last lifetime–a princess or a pea?

Where Is My Soul Mate?

My darlings, you're in fantasy! First find your soul, then perhaps you'll find your soul mate.

Check it out. Where is your Soul?? Look for it. Where is it? Is it in your ear? Perhaps it's in your nose? Maybe it's in your "heart chakra?" Or perhaps it's in your toes??? Check it out.

Close your eyes right now and search for it. Where, oh where, can it be? Maybe you've accidentally left it in a body from your last lifetime? Gee, maybe you're soul-less and are really a walk-in, an alien who took over this body? Gosh, the possibilities are endless. You could be anybody with a soul that's located somewhere.... Gee, oh gee, where can it be????

I told you. You're dreaming. I know a big deal has been made out of "the soul." Everyone refers to their inner, intuitive self as "their soul." I know you're always trying to connect with your soul and then find another soul just like you.

But, darlings, I tell you, you are definitely off the mark. You're out in La-La-Land (wherever that is). You won't ever be able to find your soul, to save your soul. You are without a doubt, soul-less. And if you doubt me, keep looking for it.

Maybe you've imagined a soul and put it in your fantasies of who you are. For what is a person without a soul? Well, according to you, he's nothing but another ant looking for a soul to crawl into, so he can evolve to the next level. With a little luck, maybe in his next life, he won't have to be an ant, because now he's got a soul. Of course, once you have a soul, you can definitely find a soul mate, whether you're an ant or not. So you're in luck, your soul mate could be right around the next corner.

Well, darlings, have you found your soul yet, the one that's waiting for your soul mate? The one the devil's been trying to get for ages? That big thing that all of creation is located in? That sacred space that houses all your karmas, dharmas, and schmarmas?

It must be there, it's got to be there somewhere in the stratosphere with all your circles, squares and triangles. Why haven't you been able to find it yet, an intelligent, devoted, spiritual person like yourself? Where is it?

My sweet adorable dears, you're hallucinating again, waiting for something that's already Here, something that's your very Nature.

Now even though "soul mate" is only a word, you've made a big deal out of it. That's why it still keeps you feeling inadequate, unable to recognize how complete and whole you already are. It keeps you in constant discontent, searching for that one possibility that will fill you up with meaning and settle your aching heart. But I tell you, darlings, you're looking for a face floating in the clouds. A phantom lover that will leave you breathless and crying for another lost chance.

However, if you're looking for somebody to love, a special friend and lover to spend the rest of your life with, then yes, go find one that suits you. One that fits best with your personality, background, likes, and dislikes. Someone that keeps you in fun and security.

But finding a "soul mate?" I don't think

so. It's a losing proposition that keeps you bound in unhappiness and expectations, looking for something that just isn't there.

So now, darlings, that you see the big fabricated soul mate paper tiger you've bought into, it's time to use your ancient mantra again, "Shut up and be happy!"

Stop breaking your head and heart over nothing. Come home to me. You can stop searching for what isn't there and come straight home to me. I'm waiting for you HERE, right in front of your face, where the devil doesn't have a chance in your ever-present precious smile.

All you have to do is smile that gorgeous, soul-less HERE smile, the one that contains everything and everybody, and you'll find your long-awaited soul mate.

When Will I Be Enlightened?

Ahh, enlightenment...that shiny brass ring you can't quite grab while you're whirling around on the merry-go-round. Your finger has brushed it a couple of times and you've even gotten your hands on it, but for some reason, you just can't hold on to it.

You're beginning to get worried that you'll never be able to catch it, and your confidence in your ability is waning. However, you see other people getting the brass ring, so you know it's possible, but somehow it's eluding you.

A little flustered, you cut your losses, listen to your family of friends around you, and decide to keep trying. You're convinced now that it's not hopeless; your timing is just off. All you need to do is be patient, go around the merry-go-round a couple more lifetimes, do all your hand and body coordination exercises, and pass all your competency tests. Then you'll have another good shot at the shiny brass ring.

Why do you want the brass ring? Because! You think the ring is magic. It will give you great powers of knowledge, bliss, happiness, control over your thoughts and emotions, health, and all around omnipotence. You'll finally be in that special, revered, minority group of great souls, who have crossed over the barrier of ordinary, miserable life.

You are going to be free and hopefully be able to fulfill all your desires. If you tend to be altruistic, maybe you'll get your parents a big house and give the world peace on earth. Otherwise, you're just going to be one cool dude.

But, darlings, I've got a surprise for you! You can't possess enlightenment. It's not an object. It's not something you can acquire by money or good deeds. You can't meditate or purify yourself enough to "reach" enlightenment. All you can do is BE enlightenment. And that's easy, because it's your very Nature—like Love, Service and Guru. It is your very Nature. It's who you are. You are Enlightenment.

Actually, it's impossible not to be enlightened. How can you not be your nature? It's your

imagination, your mind that thinks you're ignorant. You are "in" enlightenment, like everything
else.

Now, dears, I know you don't think so.
And I know you want to be free from all your
fretting and bad decisions. I see the hoops you
go through to stay on course, and I have great
love and compassion for you in your plight. I do
understand your confusion and "apparent"
dilemma.

However, darlings, you're going to have to
trust me on this one. You are enlightened. It's
impossible not to be enlightened. It's the nature
of everything. And until you wake up from this
dream, you're going to feel trapped by your own
imaginings and notions of ignorance and suffering.

So, darlings, it's time to take a break and
have a little fun. Give your enlightenment game
a rest, and set aside some of your obsessive spiritual routines that keep you blind to yourself.

Don't be so stiff and judgmental as to
what's right for your spiritual growth and everybody else's. Meditate if you want. Do asanas day

and night, if that serves you. But do it in fun and to feel better. Don't think you're going to capture the enlightenment prize because you're a big Hatha Yoga master, successful New Age teacher, intuitive psychic healer, or disciplined student who does his program regularly. Just be natural and enjoy your life.

Stop stressing about this fantasy called enlightenment. And please, oh, please, "Shut up and be happy!" You're wasting your precious time waiting for a moment in time, a brief experience that will come and go like so many thousands before. You're continually wanting to recreate a past "spiritual" experience in order to be happy and feel you're getting somewhere on "your path to enlightenment." It's a waste of good fun.

The prize that you're looking for is Here. How many times do I have to say it? It's Here. Relax, sit down and chill. You're not going to miss it. It's not going to lose you. You're not going to blow your circuits or chakras or karma. You're not going to have to start all over again as a caterpillar before you become a butterfly.

You're not going to have to buy the latest expensive enlightenment gizmo to get there faster. You only have to relax and hang out Here. The good news is you're already Here. Where else could you be?

Now, if for some unknown reason you still want to "get" enlightened, go around the merry-go-round one more time, and suffer just a little longer in the name of enlightenment, then please, get yourself a donkey. Because after hanging out with a donkey for a while, you're really going to feel enlightened–and then you can finally drop all this wearisome nonsense and just Be Happy!

Why Do I Need A Guru? How Will I Know I Found the Right One?

Darlings, the problem here is you don't have a clue as to what a Guru is. You still think he's some magician that's trying to hypnotize you into submission so he can take over your power, money and God knows what else. Maybe he wants your body—your tired, worn out, artificially pumped-up body. Boy, he really needs that to do his work in the world, especially the brain part. With your brains, he could rule the world!

Can you hear how silly you sound? It's this silly, ridiculous notion that keeps you running back to God, the omnipotent ruler of the universe. Have you ever asked yourself, "If God is ruler of the universe and the universe is finite, what is infinite?"

Of course you haven't. Because you want someone who's finite, someone like you, with a little more power, so he can get you out of tough situations. Unfortunately, God puts you into more tough situations than he gets you out of. You're actually scared to death of God, even though you're convinced He's a beneficial force.

You're constantly asking, "Why did He let bad things happen to good people? Why did the poor little girl get cancer? Why did the car accident take the parents away from their children? Why did evil win again? Why, oh why, oh why?"

Your concerns and disappointment with God are an ongoing dilemma that you can't shake. That's why there are an infinite supply of preachers and churches available to you day or night to ease your doubt. The truth is you really don't trust him, even though you've convinced yourself he's the real deal.

You're sure that your misery and misfortunate are for your own good, because you've got lessons to learn–lots and lots of lessons to learn before you can get to heaven, or reach enlightenment. You're a work in progress, suffering for a final solution that will be worth it in the end.

Frankly, I think you've been watching too much Oprah. What if I was to tell you that God is a figment of your continuous imagination?

What would you say then? Would you get offended at such an outlandish, heretical statement, or would you just walk away shaking your head at my ignorance and disbelief?

What if I told you the only lesson you have to learn is to "Shut up and be happy?" That the work in progress is finished and all you have to do is enjoy it? What would you say then?

My sweet, most adorable ones, God is a word, written in a book, painted on a canvas, hanging on a wall, in the mind of a scriptwriter. The GURU is the scriptwriter. He is all there Is. And he is the only one that can give you peace. Why? Because he is your very Nature. It's that simple.

Now, if you're lucky enough to find a Guru in the flesh, standing in front of you, calling your name, you better lay your burden down, because this is your chance to be free.

Never mind about all the questions, doubts, and nonsense you've heard. Drop your misery and step into the embrace of that sweet love That Is.

You don't ever have to worry about finding the right Guru. He will find you, and that's a promise–straight from the GURU.

"You cannot separate the
wave from the ocean."

–Sri Sri

A Final Personal Thought...

I love you. I want you to know that I always love you, regardless of your thoughts, regardless of your feelings, regardless of your moods, and regardless of your hairdo. I love you, my sweet ones.

Now that you've finished this book, it's time for a new mantra. You have no more use for that old "shut up" mantra we started with. It's time for an advanced technique, a super-charged mantra.

I would encourage you to use this mantra as often as possible, especially if you fall back into your old habits of dreaming unhappiness, blame, and doubt.

Now, my sweet ones, that you've graduated with high honors, and are going to dedicate your life to being unconditionally happy, it's time for your new mantra. Ready? Open your heart, big smile inside, and repeat after me: "Be happy!" Again, "Be happy." One more time for good measure, "Be happy." Excellent.

Now choose Me, and you'll always be Home.

In deep love,
Your friend, Dvorah

Questions and Answers

ॐ

The Nonsense That Keeps You Unhappy!

Questions and Answers
The Nonsense That Keeps You Unhappy!

Q: How come I'm always in the wrong place at the wrong time?

A: The only thing that's in the wrong place at the wrong time is your thinking. It's impossible to be in the wrong place at the wrong time. I know you've heard all this nonsense about sabotaging yourself, not listening to yourself, not being intuitive enough etc., and yada, yada, yada...but it's ridiculous. I want you to know that What Is does not make mistakes. There are no slip-ups.

You are exactly where you could "ONLY BE." So, please do not drive yourself crazy with this lament, "If only I wouldn't have been there, if only I wouldn't have done that." Drop it!!! It could not have been different. Time to learn a different mantra and say, "If it could be different, it would be different!"

Q: I believe in affirmations, they have worked for me in the past. Why don't you advocate them instead of making fun of them?

A: Look, it's not that I don't want you to do them. I just don't want you to get hooked on them as if they're a magic formula to get you what you want. It's the nature of thoughts to be just that–"thoughts that come and go." And your affirmations are thoughts that come and go, like everything else in your waking, changing dream. Sometimes thoughts manifest and sometimes they don't.

Wasting your time and your fun by constantly praying, hoping, repeating, singing and playing subliminal messages, and writing your thoughts all over the house in hopes that they'll manifest doesn't bring you peace or satisfaction. It just causes anxiety and feverishness in you, wondering when they will manifest and what you're doing wrong to keep them from manifesting.

Can you see how obsessive this thinking is? Haven't you noticed how sometimes your affirmations manifest, but most of the time they don't? And that when they don't manifest, you console yourself with thoughts like, "Maybe, when I'm enlightened enough or evolved enough, I'll be able to manifest my desires better. I just need to get more in tune with myself, more disciplined and focused. Maybe what I need is to do affirmation on getting more focused, and then I can get that red Ferrari so I can get to satsang more regularly.

This is your rationalization for spending hours, days and years being unhappy with what you don't have, hoping someday to be more abundant and fulfilled. You are wasting a perfectly happy moment, on the hopes of a better one. Please my darlings give it a rest. Stop with the useless repetitive affirmations day and night.

Maybe they'll work and maybe they won't, but either way, it is how It is—and no reason for you to lose your fun. Let life be a surprise, without your constant desire to control it. Affirmations are actually fine; like everything else that floats in and out of your mind, it's your unhappiness filled with expectations that screw it all up.

Q: All the spiritual organizations talk about "peace on earth." When will it come?

A: There are times when it's more peaceful than other times. But for the most part, peace on earth, the second coming, the age of enlightenment, the messiah and of course the Matreya are ridiculous—another way of you avoiding your joy right here and now. However, if you want to hold your breath waiting for all the promises made by your so-called "holy channels" or you want to prepare the way for your next lifetime, good luck!

I've seen you all praying for decades for the great Matreya to come. I've seen you waste your money on psychic after psychic, hoping that Merlin or Jesus will save you from the big flood, so you can be one of the chosen few to see the New Age. I've seen you chanting and playing your drums, frightened like children, in anticipation of a "second sun" lighting up the skies and possibly causing heaven or hell on earth.

If there is a fantasy that can be thought, you have thought it and made it your very own distraction. Anything and everything to worry yourself and distract yourself from What Is.

You want heaven on earth? You want peace for all mankind? You want the Second Coming? Fabulous! Then my darlings, "Shut Up and be happy!"

Q: Can I have sexual desires and still evolve and get enlightened?

A: Darling, who knows? You ask questions that are irrelevant to enlightenment. It's a happening–it's all a happening. One day you're celibate, the next day you're desiring a prostitute, and the next instant you're a free, enlightened person, living "la vida loca," completely happy and free from all your misery. One has nothing to do with the other.

But in your ignorance, you think, "If only I didn't have sexual fantasies and desire the girl next door, then I could progress on this spiritual path."

I tell you, forget it! There is nothing to

struggle with. Have a sexual desire or don't, make love or don't, either way, your enlightenment or freedom is a happening, it's a natural occurrence of finally being yourself, of finally being happy with What Is.

So again, sweet darlings, relax with all this nonsense. Just live your life and be happy. A desire comes, a desire goes, and it's nothing to get freaked out about.

Q: I'm afraid if I eat fish or chicken, I won't get enlightened. My Guru told me not to do those things, but somehow I still do. What's going to happen to me?

A: What do you think is going to happen to you? Maybe you'll turn into a chicken or a fish next lifetime and lose your chance of being enlightened for another hundred thousand million years. Come on, smarten up–different cultures eat different ways. What's considered a hindrance in one culture is pure milk and honey in another.

Now, if you've got a Guru who tells you what to do, great! Listen to Him, because it gives you peace of mind when you do. However, if it happens that you find yourself with a piece of chicken in your mouth—then, hey, swallow it, say thank you, or spit it out—either way, move on to your next meal in a couple of hours. Remember, my darlings, "If it could be different, it would be different." So, stop getting stuck on every event, and enjoy the unexpected happenings of your life, even if you don't know what you'll be doing next.

Q: My friend just recently died of cancer. She suffered a lot. I just don't get it. She seemed to do everything right (she was spiritual, prayed a lot, helped other people, loved God). Why did she suffer so much? Maybe she just didn't have enough faith?

A: See, this is the kind of thinking that keeps you miserable and in fear. First, you blame other's shortcomings for getting sick or dying, and then you worry yourself sick that you might have the same deficiency. No, it's not because she didn't have enough faith or strength or holy water. It was just her time. Do you get it? It was just her time! Now, I don't know why she suffered, and I feel great compassion for her suffering, but again, it wasn't her fault, she just did.

I know it's hard to accept that, because we want a reason for everything–but all I can say is that it was written in the script and the script was played out. All we can do is love them, meditate and pray for them, and know deep in our hearts that they are truly all right, because death and suffering are also thoughts, which are products of the mind.

Q: How can you say it doesn't get any better? I feel stronger, happier and better now than I ever have.

A: I didn't say it doesn't get better. I said it doesn't get permanently better. Things will always be changing. Today you're healthier than you've ever been, the next instant you stub your toe and are limping with a cast and feeling terrible. Things only appear to get better, but actually, YOU were always "completely fine." It's your life that continues to change from better to worse, to better to worse, ad infinitum.

Enjoy the better, but don't get stuck on wanting or expecting it to get better. Just live what comes up and know it will always change. And, darlings, don't get so apprehensive of all the changes; it can't be helped, it changes, and there is nothing you can do about it. So ride the adventure. It's usually more thrilling than most movies, because you're the leading character.

Q: I'm stuck in my meditation practice. What am I doing wrong?

A: Again with the "What am I doing wrong?" Nothing. You're doing nothing wrong. Things are always changing and that includes your meditation. Stop lamenting your loss of "great experiences" and just relax. They'll come again or they won't, but who cares? They don't mean anything anyway, you're just attached to being in a good space for an hour or so, and you love thinking you're getting somewhere on your spiritual path. Well, darlings, again, let me give you the good news! You're getting nowhere fast, with or without a vision of Krishna!

So take it as it comes and enjoy every meditation for what it is—a meditation with a lot of different experiences, period. Your expectations of "peaceful holy visions" just put you into more regret and inadequacy as a candidate for enlightenment. It's all more nonsense, full of thoughts that keep you unhappy.

So again, darlings, please, "Shut up and be happy with every meditation you have!" And remember again, for the millionth time—NO, NO, NO, you're NOT doing anything wrong! You are just doing what you're doing.

Q: What's my purpose in life?

A: You think there's a purpose out there somewhere for you, otherwise life isn't worth living. What you don't realize is that it's "you" that made a purpose necessary. It isn't part of life's equation. It's a mind glitch! It's another thought that keeps you from enjoying your life, living What Is.

Your constant search for meaning, has given you no meaning, only a never-ending search for happiness. Purpose comes and goes like everything else. One day you're on a hot new project, the next day, the project is gone and you're looking for another one to give your life meaning. Even the so-called "spiritual path" loses its "purpose" at one time or other.

Purpose in life is an illusion, an ever-changing thought that comes and goes, like everything else. But your acceptance of What Is, your chuckle in What Is—that's permanent, and your only true purpose in life.

Q: I have no discipline, how will I ever get any-where?

A: Have you ever heard the expression, "You are

not the doer?" I actually think it's an unfortunate expression, because it's so confusing. It really doesn't make any sense at all. You do, after all, "appear" to be the doer, even though all the scriptures and saints say otherwise. Why even the Buddha said, "Events happen, deeds are done, but there is no individual doer thereof."

Now, that's all very nice, but honestly it means nothing to most people, it's just a thought, another so-called "meaningful saying" to get hung up on. Why confuse yourself with all these theories? Just assume you're doing it all. However, know deeply with pure conviction that "if it could be different, it would be different!" And in fact, there is NOTHING you could have done about it! Period.

Now this thought, although like all the other thoughts floating around in your mind, will give you peace. Because now you are free to stop lamenting what you can't do, or didn't do, and start living in what's happening now. Now you have a chance at discipline and enjoying it while it lasts.

Q: You essentially said that we don't have a soul. I can buy that you are your own soul mate. But how is it possible not to have a soul? It goes against the history of Western Theology. Of course we have a soul!

A: My darlings, Open your eyes–be revolutionary! Just because someone tells you something, even someone you read about in the ancient holy books of yore, doesn't mean it's true. I can't believe how ignorant theology is–thoughts upon thoughts of ignorance and hope for the masses so they won't live and die in vain. Such total stupidity. Darling, don't you want to wake up? Isn't that why you're here? Haven't you suffered enough with someone else's fear and theories?

Be Adventurous. Be a Hero. Be the one that finally gets the awesome, incredible joke–then runs up on stage, pulls back the curtain and shows the grown-up crying children that Lassie didn't die, it was only a show.

You are greater than a word called "a soul" passing in time and space. You are Everything.

Q: I can't find a sacred place in my house to meditate or be in silence.

A: My darlings, you are silence–you don't have to go anywhere to find it. Close your eyes anywhere and you're in a sacred place. It's all sacred, every disgusting bit of this reality or any reality is sacred. It's all radiating from the same source.

So be at peace and meditate in any reality you're in. It's all your home.

Q: How can things be "only as they can be?" What happened to free will?

A: Ahh, the "free will" question. You want to exercise your free will, so you can do what? Eat pizza, instead of eggs? Or perhaps marry Jane, instead of Gertrude? This free will is very important to you, isn't it? It's that one big thing that sets you apart from the ants and turkeys and gives you your identity. You certainly don't want to be identified with a turkey.

Well, darlings, good news again—although it appears that you have free will, and you desperately want to be smart and wise enough to have free will, and you've convinced yourself with all your intellectual and spiritual knowledge that you have free will—you absolutely don't even have a smidgen of it!!!

You only "appear to be a big shaker and maker," but in truth, it's shakin' and bakin' you. It can only be, as it is, in spite of all your so-called decisions and choices. But again, even though you may know with absolute conviction that you don't have free will, it's still smart to function as if you do. Otherwise, it's just too confusing and really doesn't make sense, because the appearance of free will and making choices is so strong.

So relax. What does it matter who has free will, as long as you accept your "apparent" choices and know with deep peace that, "If it could have been different, it would have been different." Now you can go have fun, without constantly regretting your choices and boggling your mind with the concept of free will.

Q: I used to be so creative. I'm so dull now. What's happening?

A: Nothing. As usual. It's just a change, a simple second frame of the movie. Stop getting so hung up on every little change that takes place and blame yourself or something else for that change. It's the nature of life to change.

Sometimes you're creative and extraordinary, and sometimes you're not. Get used to the idea that everything is in flux and is always changing–even you. Tomorrow perhaps you'll be creative again. You don't have to run in desperation to the next seminar or healer on creativity. Relax. Everything comes full circle and happens in its own good time. Go to the beach, play with your children, watch "I Love Lucy"–but please, stop this constant yearning for the past. Be at peace with what's happening now.

Q: I used to have great meditations, what happened? It's been months and I'm still dull with the same thoughts over and over again and no peace.

A: Same thing that happened to your creativity. Again, things change all the time. It's not your fault that things change and are different. If you're meditations are lousy, go have fun in some other area of your life, or (God forbid) stop meditating for a while. Be adventurous, not so defeated. So what? So, your meditations are lousy. Big deal. Go have some fun–do a cartwheel or eat a lemon–that ought to give you a memorable experience.

Q: Why do I keep sabotaging myself? I make a plan, I promise myself I'll do it, and then I'll go do something else instead. When will I ever learn?

A: Now. Learn Now. Who told you about sabotaging yourself? Did you read it in a psychology book? Perhaps it was one of those "Seven Steps to Spiritual something or other..." Or maybe your spiritual friends are always complaining about how hard they try to stay on their path but "keep sabotaging themselves." Either way, forget it–another piece of nonsense that got stuck in your head, and now you've got to try hard to evolve to the point where you don't sabotage yourself. This is just more mind chatter that you've bought into, another theory that some Ph.D. student thought up.

How about this scenario: Sometimes you sabotage yourself and sometimes you don't, and it's all part of the cycle of your life. What you call sabotage, I call change. Sometimes it goes your way and sometimes it doesn't. And when it doesn't, you think you did something wrong. So you run to the nearest book or self-esteem seminar and try to fix yourself. And it all seems to work until next time, when you wonder what you did wrong again.

So let me repeat again: You've done nothing wrong, you're not sabotaging yourself–you're just living your life and your life changes in patterns. Be with the changes, they're natural. They're the happening of your life as it is.

Q: You keep saying, "If it could be different, it would be different." That means that everything is exactly as it can only be. Everything is right. How is that possible? How about the innocent child that's raped or the thousands that are murdered each day because they happen to live in a war zone? How can that be right? Can't we take responsibility and place blame and then demand a change? If we don't take responsibility, the atrocities and injustices will continue, and it will be our fault, my fault.

A: It is heartbreaking to see the unhappiness in the world and the "apparent" injustices. And it is heartbreaking to see the guilt and misery and blame that people live with. It's all heartbreaking–from a baby's first cry for milk to an old man's last cry for breath–life is heartbreaking. Like every classic drama, life is filled with raw emotion and every possible scenario of joy and misery in a scriptwriter's imagination. Nothing is left out in one of Tolstoy's screen dramas. And like every finished movie, once it's put on the screen of life–it is what it is.

You watch the show in awe and amazement, anticipating each new frame. Sometimes you want to change a story line, but you can't alter the movie from where you're sitting in the audience. All you can do is watch the show–sometimes with tears of joy and laughter, and sometimes with tears of horror, fear and anxiety. Either way–it is what it is–and you're helpless to do anything about it, except stay for the ride until the movie is over.

In life, when tragedy strikes, you're also in for a ride that you can't change. You feel helpless, and you curse your fate and your circumstances. "If only I could do something, if only I could change my prior actions, maybe I could change the outcome," you cry.

But, I tell you, this feeling of helplessness is your greatest blessing and ticket to peace. The more helpless you feel and the less you struggle to change what can't be changed, the closer you are to accepting the exquisite, peaceful truth of, "If it could be different, it would be different." Then you could stop blaming yourself and others and finally drop the bitter heavy load you've been carrying of guilt, regret, and "if only's."

War and all the other atrocities in life are

what they are–the unfortunate horror of a particular drama, a natural happening. If your character is one that works towards alleviating misery and injustice, then you will focus your life in that direction–serving where you can, offering what you can. However, you will only do what your character is structured to do, what is possible for you to do.

Now, if you want to do your part and serve efficiently in this world without freaking out every time it doesn't go your way, or doesn't go well in general, you will need to go into the depth and presence of your new "Serenity" mantra. And with a full helpless heart know–"If it could be different, it would be different."

Q: How do I combine my spiritual life with raising a family? I don't have time to meditate, and the kids are always taking me out of my peaceful state.

A: You are Peace. Relax. Your very nature is peace and spirituality. Meditate when you can and don't worry about it when you can't.

Meditation may make you feel more peaceful, or not, but either way–it's another "cool thing" that you do. Enjoy it when you can and the rest of the time have fun with your family and kids. This is your life, the only one you've got right now. Be with it. And remember, "You don't get spiritual, you are spiritual already–it's your very nature."

Q: You're always talking about "the waking dream" or it "appears to be." What are you talking about?

A: Things are not always as they seem. I was sitting on my sofa one day when the colors of the rainbow appeared on my hand. I looked at my hand, and it really looked as if those colors were permanently painted on. However, when I moved my hand they disappeared, because the sun's reflection didn't shine there anymore. Yet, when I put my hand back in the light, the rainbow appeared, and the colors again "appeared" permanent.

Appearances can be deceiving. Some things that appear permanent are in flux and in changing illusion. We appear to be moving on stable flat ground, but in reality, we're moving in space. You're standing on top of the world walking around in pure space. If gravity didn't hold you down, you couldn't walk to the nearest Starbucks. You'd be floating in space without your cup of coffee.

In the same way, we appear to be living a meaningful life full of joys, disappointments and purpose. And we appear to be in the school of life, moving towards enlightenment or preparing for the life hereafter, or whatever...but the appearance is far different from The Real. The truth is unimaginable and impossible for your mind to comprehend. You'll have to go beyond your mind into the deep space of What Is to recognize the waking dream and fathom the incomprehensible illusion of the hypnotic Divine Maya.

Meanwhile, my darlings, relax. This life, your waking dream, is up for re-examination and discovery. Somewhere along the line, you'll notice a rainbow reflection on your own hand, and wonder very deeply how it came to look so permanent?

Q: According to many well-known New Age thinkers and healers, you're not in control of the events that happen to your life, but you're in control of how you deal with those events. That suggests a degree of control and free will. Could you comment on that?

A: Honestly, I don't know what they're talking about. It's sounds like goobly-goop to me, another theory to peddle to people so they can feel safe and in control. THAT which structured the events, also structured how you dealt with those events. You'll notice that when unexpected things happen to you, regardless of your spiritual or psychological training, you'll deal with things differently each time. Sometimes you handle things well and sometimes you don't. Either way, relax with the results of your attitude or actions. It is what it is. The events couldn't be different and your thinking and reactions couldn't be different. So forget all this third-rate psychological mind manipulation to feel safe and in control. In reality, you're already safe and the Big Kahuna is in control.

Q: I know it's all a waking dream, I know no one ever dies, but my son was killed in an accident a year ago and he was all alone when it happened. I can't seem to get that image out of my mind, and my knowledge falls flat when I think of him. What can I do?

A: Do the Art of Living Course—and darling, know you're loved. That Big Beautiful Peace that you are has enveloped you and your son. Both are safe in the arms of What Is.

Q: I'm scared of my anger. I don't know what I would do if I didn't harness it.

A: It's your fear of getting angry that's driving you crazy, not the anger itself. When was the last time you harnessed anything? Did you stop yourself before saying that stupid thing, or did it just come out? Did you stop yourself from getting angry when your husband left the toothpaste out? If you examine your anger, you'll see that sometimes you could harness it and sometimes you couldn't.

You're going to have to trust me on this one, and relax. Don't get so caught up in what you do. Do the best you can, and then relax and move on to the next moment without the same old mind tape of misery and regret. Say, "I'm sorry," try not to do it again, and continue with your daily adventure.

Q: Why can't everyone be more loving? If they would just try a little harder, the world wouldn't be in such a mess.

A: Darling, have you tried to be more loving? I assume you have. Has it worked? If it has, congratulations. Now go out and try to force everyone else to be more loving. Does it work? Is it a loving thing to do? Are people more loving due to your efforts? Don't bother to try and change others–just try being loving with yourself. If your mission in life is to be more loving, go for it–but leave others alone.

The world isn't in a mess because "we're" not more loving. The world is in a mess because that's what the world does...it goes in and out of messes. Our job and peace is to accept the mess. However, if your system is inclined to clean up the mess, then you'll be out there with shovels and peanut butter sandwiches, helping the mess police...and that can be a very loving thing to do, instead of forcing others to be more loving.

Q: You said people don't have a purpose? Do Gurus have a purpose? I read my Guru is here for a mission, that his mission is to bring a certain number of "souls" back Home.

A: Darlings, I'm blown away by your desire to

believe everything you read. Where is home? And what happens if he doesn't meet his quota? Do "they," whoever they are, take away his Gurudom? What nonsense! The Guru is every-thing–absolutely everything. He doesn't have to "do" anything; He is everything. Home is our very nature, it's not some place to go. It's WHO WE ARE!

Believe what you want, but why fill your mind with other people's old stories, when dis-covering your own story is so much more fun and meaningful. Discover the Guru for yourself. Write your own Guru stories.

Q: I heard that my Guru is the reincarnation of Krishna, Jesus, and Shiva. He hasn't denied it, so it must be true. Can you comment on this?

A: Let me say it again. The Guru is Everything. Past, present and future. So, if you want to call him Krishna, Jesus, Shiva, Shankara or Pancho Villa, be my guest. How about discovering who the Guru is for yourself?

It's so boring and easy to say, "Yep, there's Jesus again," or "Yep, there's Krishna dancing with his gopis again." Why not wonder about this vast blissful sight and presence called "the Guru?" Be a little adventurous. Grow some...(you know what I mean), or at least grow some mistletoe and kiss yourself under it. Think about something outrageous instead of the same old recycled religious and spiritual fabrications. Wake up!!! It's time to delight in the fragrance of newly discovered roses.

Q: How can you say that we don't learn lessons before we become enlightened? In the Bible, there's the story of Job and the lessons he had to learn. And even Jesus had to go through his trials before he came to God. What do you have to say about this?

A: Nothing. Darlings, believe what you want, what else can you do? However, if you're asking me, I say, "Shut up and be happy!" Why in heaven's name would God need to test you? He is everything, knows everything about you and what you're capable of, why would he need to test you? Think about it. Honestly, it just doesn't make any sense. It's your imagination again playing old tapes from the archives of past memories. Drop all this barrage of useless thoughts and come into the cool, vast freshness of the Here and Now.

No one is testing you. You're free to have fun and live your life without this constant nagging discomfort, feelings of inadequacy and struggle. You're Here. You're already free, and you passed the tests before you were ever born. Now live in peace. It's your very Nature.

Q: One more question. If in fact peace is our very nature, why are we so restless?

A: Because.

Much love to you all, Dvorah

Quotes by Sri Sri
(from *Seeds of Wisdom*)

"Silence is the totality of mind—in it, the other disappears. Be quiet for awhile."

"You are solidified silence, awareness. A thousand hours of speech cannot equal one glance; a hundred glances cannot equal one minute of silence."

"Liberation from society means liberation from words."

"Unpleasant experiences come and go. Accept them with the power of the Self."

"Laugh and make others laugh. Don't get entangled and don't entangle others."

"Desire for the One leads to the One. Many are a mess."

"Let go of all efforts, search and desires, for He can be felt only in deep peace and stillness."

"Be with opposites—dance with them."

"Be neither doer or non-doer."

"There is no such thing as a flawless action, but there is such a thing as a flawless actor."

"Vision is what gives direction to life energy—doing. A mistake is an action disconnected from the vision. Do not slip from your vision."

About the Author

Dvorah Adler has a M.A. in Human Development and a B.A. in Early Childhood Education. She was a featured columnist for the Chicago Tribune Women News and has hosted her own TV and radio shows on Enlightened Parenting and other radical topics in the field of Human Development.

She has been teaching meditation and talking about personal freedom all over the United States for the past 33 years. Presently she lives in Ojai and is extremely happy.

You can contact Dvorah through her website:
www.momscomefirst.com

Other books by Dvorah

Moms Come First!
Three Steps to Enlightened Parenting

"My Little Guru"
and Other Wonderous Adventure
Stories, and Divine Quotes of LOVE

Dvorah's website:
www.momscomefirst.com

Recommendations for the Body and Mind

Art of Living Course Part l

The Art of Living Foundation welcomes you to a joyous, practical, transforming weekend of experience and knowledge designed by His Holiness Sri Sri Ravi Shankar. The holistic, health-giving techniques taught in this course eliminate stress, increase energy, and improve your vitality and joy in life. Your true nature is revealed. You find your center and wholeness in life.

A broad range of processes offered include:

• Sudarshan Kriya–Centerpiece of the course and a powerful method that allows awareness to open and stimulates healing. It increases harmony within the body, mind, and spirit.

• Purna Yoga—Simple, easy yoga postures that center and rejuvenate the body and mind.

• Pranayama—Breathing techniques that help you consciously govern your breath to enhance and increase Prana, the life-giving vitality within your Self.

• Living in the Present—Easy and enjoyable processes that open your awareness to live fully in the present moment, without past regrets or future apprehension.

This relaxing course is fun and easy. Anyone can do it. There is no conflict with any other religious or spiritual practices. What is learned on the course is easily practiced at home every day.

For more information, please call:
1-877-399-1008
or visit website: **www.artofliving.org**

Sahaj Samadhi Meditation Course

"Unless one settles into the depth of one's Being, the truth will not be revealed." –Sri Sri

Meditation is a natural state that may be experienced even without a specific technique. It could be a moment of love or joy, or a flash of transcendence during a beautiful sunset. But to experience this on a regular basis, a technique is desirable.

Sahaj Samadhi Meditation is a natural, effortless, and graceful practice that offers deep relaxation, energy, and spiritual awakening to people of all backgrounds and traditions. It takes just a few sessions to learn, and you continue to practice it at home twice a day, for about twenty minutes each time.

Sahaj is a Sanskrit word that means "natural." Samadhi means "pure awareness" or "highest bliss." In Sahaj Samadhi, the mind effortlessly transcends surface thinking to experience the depth of its own nature. No concentration or control is involved, just the mind's own nature to move towards greater happiness. In this settled state, your awareness expands, perception and emotions become refined, and the body gains a deep purifying and healing rest.

With regular meditation, benefits of deep rest and expanded awareness extend throughout the day into your everyday activity, bringing greater ease, clarity and fulfillment in life.

For more information, please call:
1-877-399-1008
or visit website: **www.artofliving.org**

For more information about Art of Living courses, workshops, and programs, contact a center closest to you:

AFRICA

Hema & Rajaraman

Art of Living

P.O. Box 1213

Peba Close Plot 5612

Gaborone, Botswana

Tel. 26-735-2175

Aolbot@global.co.za

CANADA

Fondation L'Art de Vivre

B.P. 170

13 Chemin du lac Blanc

St. Mathieu-du-Parc, Quebec   GOX 1NO

Tel. 819-532-3328

Artofliving.northamerica@sympatico.ca

GERMANY

Akadamie Bad Antogast
Bad Antogast 1
77728 Oppenau
Germany
Tel. 49-7804-910-923
Artofliving.Germany@t-online.de

INDIA

Vyakti Vikras Kendra, India
No. 19, 39th A Cross,
11th Main
4th T block, Jayanagar
Bangalore 560041, India
Tel. 91-80-6645106
vvm@vsnl.com

UNITED STATES

Art of Living Foundation
P.O. Box 50003
Santa Barbara, CA 93150
Tel. 877-399-1008
www.artofliving.org

Art of Living Foundation
Service Programs

The Art of Living Foundation (www.artofliving.org), established by His Holiness Sri Sri Ravi Shankar, is an international nonprofit educational and humanitarian organization. It is active in over 140 countries. The foundation is dedicated to bringing peace to individuals and fostering human values within the global community.

The International Association for Human Values (www.iahv.org) is also founded by Sri Sri Ravi Shankar. IAHV's mission is to promote and support the development of human values. Through a variety of educational activities and service projects aimed at social transformation, IAHV works to restore peace and harmony for all. IAHV in collaboration with Art of Living Foundation is assisting in the Tsunami-relief effort. Over 440 tons of materials have been collected and distributed so far. Over 3500 people have been given courses to help them deal with the trauma and stress. Lots more is being done daily.

The 5H Program (www.5h.org) involves volunteers in social and community development projects with a focus on Health, Homes, Hygiene, Human values, and Harmony in diversity. Because addressing physical needs alone can neither result in long-term eradication of poverty nor bring about a fundamental social transformation, the 5H program adopts a holistic approach to social development. Current programs are in Belize, India, Indonesia, Iran, Iraq, Mexico, Poland and the United States.

Other service projects include: Care for Children, women and rural empowerment projects, Prison Smart, literacy, health care and many others. For more information or how you can help, please contact the Art of Living Foundation.

Sri Sri Ayurveda
(Health & Balance of Life)

Ayurveda, "the science of healing," is the natural and the most ancient known healing system. It encompasses all aspects of human life from the biological to the spiritual. It provides an integrated approach for preventing and treating illness through potent herbal formulations, lifestyle interventions and natural therapies. It is based on the view that the elements, forces, and principles that comprise all of nature–and that holds it together and make it function–are also seen in human beings. Ayurveda takes a holistic view, wherein laws of nature are equally applicable to a human being.

Ayurveda is made up of two Sanskrit words: Ayu, which means life, and Veda, which means the knowledge of. To know about life is Ayurveda. Ayurveda is a holistic system of healing which evolved among the sages of ancient India some 3000-5000 years ago. Historical evidence of Ayurveda in the ancient books of wisdom known as the Vedas has been validated. Ayurveda is a system that helps maintain health in a person by using the inherent principles of nature to bring the individual back into equilibrium with their true self.

1. It focuses on establishing and maintaining balance of the life energies within us, rather than focusing on individual symptoms.

2. It recognizes the unique constitutional differences of all individuals and therefore recommends different regimens for different types of people. Although two people may appear to have the same outward symptoms, their energetic constitutions may be very different and therefore call for very different remedies.

3. It is a complete medical system, which recognizes that ultimately all intelligence and wisdom flow from one Absolute source. Ayurveda assists Nature by promoting harmony between the individual and Nature by living a life of balance according to her laws.

website: www.srisriayurved.com

Sri Sri Yoga

"Like a flower bud, human life has the potential to blossom fully. Blossoming of human potential to fullness is yoga."

–Sri Sri

It is an inherent desire in humans to be happy. The ancient sages, through inquiry about life, were able to reach a state of consciousness in which the secrets of healthier, happier and meaningful living were revealed to them. Sages called that secret and sacred knowledge "yoga."

The term "yoga" is derived from the Sanskrit word "yuj," meaning union, the union of the individual consciousness with the universal Consciousness. The knowledge of yoga can be found in ancient scriptures dating back over 5000 years.

Yoga transcends any religion or culture. Its application is universal. Yoga is not merely a form of exercise for the body, but a path towards total harmony of body, mind and spirit. It is ancient wisdom for a healthier, happier and more peaceful way of living that ultimately leads to Self-realization, the union with the Self.

Sri Sri Yoga is a balanced discipline, which offers a multi-path approach for uniting body, breath and mind with awareness. Sri Sri Yoga brings you the wisdom and techniques of yoga in a very joyful, sincere and thorough manner. A combination of gentle and vigorous series of asanas is taught for the well-being of the body, while an equal emphasis is placed on techniques for nurturing the mind and spirit.

contact@srisriyoga.info